"Beyond the theological richness, psychological soundness, and tried-and-true practicality of *Parenting in the Pastorate*, its author, Paul Gilbert, together with his wife, Susan, are the real deal! I know, because my wife and I are good friends of theirs. We assure you the Gilberts know what they're talking about and are trustworthy guides through this wild and wonderful adventure of parenting!"

Gregg Allison, Professor of Christian Theology, The Southern Baptist Theological Seminary

"It's a rare find to read a book that is both rich in Scriptural wisdom and completely accessible to 'normal' people. Paul Gilbert has pulled that off. This little book is a wonderful guide for parents who wish to have practical advice for navigating a family through the trials and tribulations of pastoral life. Especially helpful is the section on the inevitability of the church in the life of raising families. 'The church is God's forever family,' says Gilbert, and we all would be the better to remember as much in a world defined by expressive individualism. A real gift to God's people."

Les Newsom, Lead Pastor, Christ Presbyterian Church, Oxford, MS

"Paul and Susan Gilbert have produced a wonderfully written, easily accessed, and powerful manual on practical parenting. While written primarily for couples engaged in full-time ministry, it will greatly benefit all parents who want to see Christ formed in their children. The illustrations are captivating, the writing is engaging, but more importantly, the principles and practical advice will leave you thinking 'that's just what I needed!' If you're a parent now, or hoping to be, buy this book. If your children are grown and headed for parenthood gift this book to them for the sake of your grandkids. And lastly, if you love your pastor and his family, give him this a book and a $50 bill, and send him and his wife on a nice dinner date. They'll thank you, and so will their kids."

Dr. David W. Hegg, Senior Pastor, Grace Baptist Church, Santa Clarita, CA; Adjunct Professor, The Master's University; and author of *The Obedience Option; Appointed to Preach;* and *When My Heart Is Faint*

Praise for the "How-To" Series

"The Sojourn Network 'How-To' books are a great combination of biblical theology and practical advice, driven by a commitment to the gospel and the local congregation. Written by the local church for the local church — just the job!"

> **Tim Chester**, pastor of Grace Church Boroughbridge, faculty member of Crosslands Training, and author of over 40 books

"This series brings pastoral wisdom for everyday life in the church of Jesus Christ. Think of these short, practical books as the equivalent of a healthy breakfast, a sandwich and apple for lunch, and a family enjoying dinner together. The foundational theology is nutritious, and the practical applications will keep the body strong."

> **Dr. David Powlison**, Executive Director of CCEF; senior editor, Journal of Biblical Counseling; author of *Good and Angry: Redeeming Anger* and *Making All Things New: Restoring Joy to the Sexually Broken*

"Most leaders don't need another abstract book on leadership; we need help with the 'how-to's.' And my friends in the Sojourn Network excel in this area. I've been well served by their practical ministry wisdom, and I know you will be too."

> **Bob Thune**, Founding Pastor, Coram Deo Church, Omaha, NE, author of *Gospel Eldership* and co-author of *The Gospel-Centered Life*

"I cannot express strong enough what a valuable resource this is for church planters, church planting teams and young churches. The topics that are addressed in these books are so needed in young churches. I have been in ministry and missions for over 30 years and I learned a lot from reading. Very engaging and very practical!"

Larry McCrary, Co-Founder and Director of The Upstream Collective

"There are many aspects of pastoral ministry that aren't (and simply can't) be taught in seminary. Even further, many pastors simply don't have the benefit of a brotherhood of pastors that they can lean on to help them navigate topics such as building a healthy plurality of elders or working with artists in the church. I'm thankful for the men and women who labored to produce this series, which is both theologically-driven and practically-minded. The Sojourn Network "How-To" series is a great resource for pastors and church planters alike."

Jamaal Williams, Lead Pastor of Sojourn Midtown, Louisville, KY

"HOW-TO" FAITHFULLY RAISE
KIDS IN FULL-TIME MINISTRY

Parenting

◄ IN ►
THE
PASTORATE

Paul Gilbert

Series Editor: Dave Harvey

Parenting in the Pastorate
"How-To" Faithfully Raise Kids in Full-Time Ministry

© 2019 Paul Gilbert
All rights reserved.

A publication of Sojourn Network Press in Louisville, KY. For more books by Sojourn Network, visit us at sojournnetwork.com/store.

Cover design: Josh Noom & Benjamin Vrbicek
Interior design: Benjamin Vrbicek

Trade paperback ISBN: 978-1732055292

The Sojourn Network book series is dedicated to the pastors, elders, and deacons of Sojourn Network churches. Because you are faithful, the church will be served and sent as we plant, grow, and multiply healthy churches that last.

CONTENTS

SERIES PREFACE

Why should the Sojourn Network publish a "How-To" series?

It's an excellent question, since it leads to a more personal and pertinent question for you: *Why should you bother to read any of these books?*

Sojourn Network, the ministry I am honored to lead, exists to plant, grow, and multiply healthy networks, churches, and pastors. Therefore, it seems only natural to convert some of our leader's best thinking and practices into written material focusing on the "How-To" aspects of local church ministry and multiplication.

We love church planters and church planting. But we've come to believe it's not enough to do assessments and fund church plants. We must also help, equip, and learn from one another in order to be good shepherds and leaders. We must stir up one another to the good work of leading churches towards their most fruitful future.

That's why some books will lend themselves to soul calibration for ministry longevity, while others will examine the riggings of specific ministries or specialized mission. This is essential work to building ministries *that last*. But God has also placed it on our hearts to share our mistakes and most fruitful practices so that others might improve upon what we have done. This way, everyone wins.

If our prayer is answered, this series will bring thoughtful, pastoral, charitable, gospel-saturated, church-grounded, renewal-based "practice" to the rhythms of local church life and network collaboration.

May these "How-To" guides truly serve you. May they arm you with new ideas for greater leadership effectiveness. Finally, may they inspire you to love Jesus more and serve his people with grace-inspired gladness, in a ministry that passes the test of time.

Dave Harvey
President, Sojourn Network

INTRODUCTORY LETTER

Dear Ministry Parent,

One of my favorite movies is *The Perfect Storm*. Based loosely upon a true story, George Clooney plays deep-sea fisherman, Captain Billy Tyne, who makes his living snagging swordfish off the coast of New England. A hard-working, dedicated father and husband, Tyne decides to take his crew on a last, end-of-the-season run in hopes of securing a final catch before winter sets in.

What transpires next is a tragic confluence of events that effectively dooms the *Andrea Gail*, Tyne's fishing trawler. A hurricane, two different extreme weather fronts, a rogue wave, and a broken ice machine all conspire to send the *Andrea Gail* to the bottom of the ocean.

What is fascinating is that in and of themselves, none of these unexpected developments would have been enough to sink this vessel. However, in combination, the resulting perfect storm of factors made survival almost impossible.

In many ways, we pastors and wives are like Billy Tyne. We are seeking to be faithful and fruitful in our ministries, marriages, and families, but are largely unaware that a perfect storm is brewing just offshore. And, this maelstrom threatens to send our own pastoral vessels down to the bottom of the sea.

Sadly, it is often our children who end up being the causes or the casualties of such a storm.

Recently, I spoke with a long-time pastor friend who had made the decision to permanently leave the ministry. The reason? The stresses, strains, and suffering that his family endured as part of the warp and woof of pastoral ministry were too much to bear. His children had suffered enormously, and it was time to remove them from the fishbowl of ministry.

Another pastoral colleague decided to resign his position for a different but related reason: the behavior of his children revealed a "management of household" qualification issue. He simply was not able to effectively attend to both the affairs of the church and the challenges of parenting at the same time. Thus, his vocational ministry life came to a sad close.

The moral of the story? Both pastoral and parenting pressures, each significant in their own right, can conspire to create a perfect storm that threatens both the livelihoods and the lives of pastors and their families.

Why is being a parent in full-time, vocational ministry so challenging? Here are just a few reasons:

21st Century Parenting

James Dobson wrote a book several decades back entitled *Parenting Isn't for Cowards*. Dobson was right then, and he's even more right now. Parenting children in our sex-saturated, technology-immersed, relativistic culture is a full-time, 24/7 endeavor in ways that it has never been before. This is the default, cultural milieu into which the Christian pastor and parent ventures forth.

Ecclesiastical Expectations

Let's face it, people in our churches and ministries have expectations for what a pastor's family should and should not be doing. This can create enormous pressure on pastors, wives, and children alike to behave and act in certain ways. Sometimes, though, these ways are not necessarily congruent with a family's gifts, personalities, callings, and spiritual lives. The subtle and not so subtle preconceived notions about roles and expectations for "the first families of the church" are enough to send many children careening off course.

The P. K. Syndrome

Closely related to the aforementioned factor, "Pastor's Kid" can become the primary identity marker for a child. Even mentioning the P.K. moniker can conjure up nightmares of out of control church children doing their part to make sure no one mistakes them for what they truly are! This, of course, is a recipe for hypocrisy, acting out, and inauthentic relating, which can be catastrophic for the church — and especially for the child.

The Tension of Time

If you ask pastors and their spouses to name their 3 greatest challenges in church work, surely seeking a proper balance between family and ministry would be among them.

The tasks of both parenting and pastoring seem to be endless and ongoing. To say "yes" to one means saying "no" to the other. The nagging, guilty feeling that nothing is ever enough is an ongoing, unresolved tension.

Where We're Coming From

Susan and I have been married for 26 plus years and have 4 children. We currently have the challenge of raising children who are somewhere on the spectrum between mature adulthood and middle school. We came into the ministry without any children, and by God's grace we hope to remain in ministry long after the children have gone.

We have been in full-time pastoral ministry for the last 23 years at one church filling various roles: youth, college, adult, counseling, small groups, executive pastor, and now lead pastor. These two decades plus have seen our church go through countless ups and downs, including two lead pastor transitions; the moral failing of a key leader; the planting/launching of three new congregations; several building projects and campaigns; and a financial crisis or three.

So, do all of these things qualify us to write a book on parenting in the pastorate? Well, not exactly.

We are two broken people living in a loving but imperfect marriage, attempting to shepherd four loving but imperfect children. We have been the benefactors of God's amazing grace in the fruit we have seen in our children's lives, and we thank him for it. Oftentimes, this fruit seems to have been produced not because of our parenting but in spite of it!

What we wish to do in this book is to simply share some of the things that God has chosen to bless in our parenting and other things that he has not, and to highlight the goodness and wisdom that he gives to us parents through his Word.

How to Use This Book

One thing you might want to do before plowing through this book is for you and your spouse to go out for a cup of coffee and do a spiritual audit on your parenting. What's going well; what's not? What do you thank God for, and what are you praying for Him to change? Are there areas of disunity in your parenting? What have been some of your biggest parental "wins"? "Losses"?

Once you have done this, start to scan some of the topics and sections of this book, reflecting on what sort of thoughts, fears, or anxieties they raise. Begin to pray together as a couple about what God might be doing in your hearts.

Then, it would be helpful for each of you to read through the book on your own and then come back together to share your thoughts and observations. It is here that you will want to start praying over and discussing small "chunks" or sections of the book.

To help you organize your thoughts, discussion, prayers, and application, here is how the book is laid out:

Philosophy: Gospel-Grounded Parenting — We will set the foundation of the parenting enterprise squarely upon the Good News that Jesus Christ died not only for the sins of our children but for our failures as parents as well.

Principles: Parental Building Blocks — What are the "parenting pillars" that we want to set in place that will give shape to everything we do with our kids? This section will examine 5 of these building blocks.

Process: The Priorities of Parenting — This last section seeks to spell out three specific priorities that function as "headers" under which we can file the main things we want to be doing as ministry parents.

Finally, there will be a **Practice** section in the Appendix that will leave you with a few hands-on resources as you seek to parent in the pastorate.

As fellow parents, we are praying for you as you seek to faithfully and fruitfully shepherd your two flocks: your children and your church.

Grace and Peace,
Paul and Susan Gilbert

PHILOSOPHY

GOSPEL-GROUNDED PARENTING

Many people would say that marriage is the most heart-revealing and soul-exposing relationship on planet earth. Indeed, there have been times in our marriage of where this has certainly felt true. However, Susan and I were blessed with three years of dating where we were able to build a shared vision together before deciding to say, "I do." These 36 months proved to be the rich soil we needed to grow something truly special and long-lasting.

It doesn't exactly work that way with parenting and kids.

Our first child, Grace, was born on February 7, 1999. However, she did not join our family after a long history of us swapping back-stories and deciding together that we were the right fit. Quite the opposite, Grace was dropped into our lives as a complete unknown. Her temperament, personality, quirks, faith, and dreams were all sovereign surprises that have been unwrapped, one day at a time, over the last 20 years.

Susan and I truly love our four kids. They are amazing, awesome, and well, just throw in every other descriptive adjective that you can imagine. But let's be clear about something: it's been nearly impossible to predict how *their* genetic makeups would interact and sync with *our* genetic makeups. Unlike deciding whom to marry, we had no input or control over the types of children that would join the Gilbert family for the rest of our lives.

This is why we would say that being a parent, quite possibly above all other human relationships, ruthlessly exposes a person's brokenness, sinfulness, and self-orientation. Parenting itself carries thousands of complexities that leave us feeling, at times, nothing less than desperate. Thus, parents are going to be acutely aware of their own weaknesses and shortcomings.

While you may do most of your book ordering online, the next time you venture into one of those brick and mortar bookstore chains, try this out: cruise by the Parenting/Children section and feast your eyes on the veritable smorgasbord of resources. It's not that there are just hundreds and hundreds of books on parenting — it's that there are dozens and dozens of books on dozens and dozens of specific parenting issues. Discipline, child development; ADHD, anxiety, OCD, learning, cognitive advancement, and step-parenting are but a few of the topics that are represented on these shelves.

And, before we proceed further, let us say unequivocally that this *can be* a great thing. The knowledge base, research, study, and medical advances made in many of these areas have proven invaluable to parents. Even Christian parents in the ministry, like us!

A few years back, Susan and I began noticing water pooling up sporadically in our garage and utility room. With kids in the house, this is not an uncommon occurrence, and we chalked it up to wet clothes left out or everyone's lunch boxes not being emptied out over the weekend. However, just as soon as we would clean up the liquid, it would reappear. Magically, almost.

Now, call us obtuse, but we didn't think much about it and kept this process going for a few days. Or, maybe it was a few weeks. Eventually, though, we discovered the source of the water: a leak behind the refrigerator that ended up putting us out of the house for 6 weeks for mold remediation and extensive repair work.

Sometimes, Christian parenting can function like this. We attack the presenting problem with gusto, but if we are not careful, we will go to work on the symptoms without addressing the source. And, the water will keep pumping out of the refrigerator faster than we can clean it up.

The moral of the story: as important as techniques, programs, or plans are in helping our children, they are not nearly as effective when they don't receive the proper priority. Parents need something sturdier, something theologically sound, something deeper to draw from, both for ourselves and for our children.

This "something" may or may not surprise you. This "something" is the gospel.

As believers, it is tempting to think of the gospel as a static body of information that saved us at conversion and will one day, when we enter eternity, be useful again. In this way of thinking, the gospel is like a raft we sit inside as we paddle feverishly through a Class VI whitewater rapid. It delivers us safely to the end, but we have to cooperate with God by adding an enormous amount of sweat and effort on our part to make it.

As parents, we can sometimes fall prey to this same way of thinking. We affirm the truths of the gospel but overlook how it drills down into the "how-to's" of our parenting. Our burden is that we not only be schooled in the *content* of the gospel but in the *application* of the gospel. This is particularly important when it comes to parenting. Not just in the way we parent our kids, but also in the way we look at ourselves. Let's begin there.

The Gospel-Shaped Parent

Scripture is so real. For instance, it might surprise you to discover that the Apostle Peter struggled to live out the practicalities of the gospel. In Acts 10, Peter comes to understand that the gospel allowed both Jews and Gentiles to enjoy equal standing before God and also before each other. However, just a short time later, some Judaizers from Jerusalem arrived in Galatia and refused to treat the Gentile Christians as their spiritual equals. They even declined to eat meals with them.

Peter, unfortunately, switched allegiances and followed their lead by treating his Gentile brothers as second-class citizens. This spiritual schizophrenia created division, anger, and hurt within the church community.

Now, let's think about this. Who would argue that Peter did not intellectually understand the truths of the gospel? He was an apostle, after all! Peter, though, failed to live consistently with the truths of the gospel. He neglected to apply them to his relationships because he was basically living in fear of what the Judaizers would think of him (Galatians 2:14).

I don't know about you, but Susan and I find that our parenting is often driven by the same kind of gospel-denying, fear-of-man dynamic that afflicted Peter. It can take many forms and show up in unexpected ways:

- **Discipline:** "If I confront my teenager, will they still like me?"
- **Boundaries:** "If I say, 'No,' to this activity that "all" the other kids are participating in, will other families think we are strange?"
- **Helicoptering:** "If I allow my child to fail, will other people think we are terrible parents?"

In the hit TV sitcom *The Wonder Years*, Kevin Arnold, on the heels of failing to defend the nerd of the class, Margaret Barkwahr, because of his fear of what the other boys would think of him, rather astutely says, "Who you are in 8th grade is who other 8th graders say that you are." We would venture to say that the same thing is often true for us as parents: Who we are as parents is often defined by who other people say that we are.

> **Who we are as parents is often defined by who other people say that we are.**

The gospel of grace is the only solution to combating these kinds of fears. Specifically, parents need to keep running to a gospel that declares:

- Our successes and failures as parents do not change our relationship with Christ
- My security and significance as a person is based upon what Christ has done for me, not what I have (or have not) accomplished as a parent
- Spiritual victories in parenting are a testimony to God's grace
- Spiritual defeats in parenting are a reminder of our ongoing need of that grace

The gospel gives us the courage and the spiritual cover to humbly celebrate our successes and boldly admit our failures. To paraphrase a thought often attributed to Tim Keller, the glorious gospel reminds us that we are more broken and sinful than we could ever truly know, but we are also simultaneously more loved and forgiven than we could ever conceive. The gospel — the truth that Jesus died for us and rose from the grave for us — tells us that our performance, self-worth, and value as parents is ultimately tied to Christ's love, not to how well we parent. For any man or woman with kids, that's good news indeed!

The Gospel-Shaped Child

Ask any pastor and his wife about their hearts' deepest desires for their children, and the response will almost certainly be immediate and instinctual: "We want our children to love the Lord, to trust in Him, and to walk faithfully in his ways." I know that is the way Susan and I have often prayed for our children. The most foundational piece of this equation, of course, is that our children would embrace the truths of the gospel and place their faith in Jesus. In doing so, they come to be identified, just as all Christians are, as a new creation in Christ — the old has passed away, the new has come.

Here is the challenge, though, particularly for children growing up in the confines of full-time, pastoral ministry. From the moment that they set foot into the world or the church building, these children begin to take on a distinctive identity that seems to trump their most basic identities as a human being or Christian.

Most of us are probably familiar with the PK (i.e., "Pastor's Kid") label that is often slapped on the proverbial backs of children who grow up with parents in full-time ministry. The term itself is one laden with enough expectations, fears, concerns, and bad memories to send the average member running to the sanctuary balcony for cover. What church member hasn't heard or narrated their own horror stories of pastor's kids gone wild?

This reputation for ecclesiastical unruliness has been undoubtedly well-earned by many children of pastors growing up in the church. In fact, many pastors have felt compelled to resign their ministry positions due to the rebellion of their children and their parental inability to control rebellious behavior. While there is considerable debate about what it means for an elder to have an orderly and submissive home, one thing is not debatable: P.K.'s can feel responsible for dad's livelihood.

No one likes the feeling that they are being used — whether it be in politics, dating, or the workplace. This is particularly true for the P. K. — he or she understands if they are being parented and loved for who they are versus who their parents need them to be. Understandably, pastor's kids can become bitter and resentful when they perceive that they are the means to some other goal.

While not necessarily being conscious of the shift, pastoral parents can become more concerned about the state of the church vs. the state of their child's heart. Spiritual qualifications for ministry become the incentive for shepherding a child's heart, versus spiritual qualifications being the by-product of faithfully shepherding a child's heart.

And, a pastor's kid can smell the difference from a mile away. For a generation of kids being raised in the "Era of Authenticity," they can become particularly sensitive to hypocrisy. P. K.'s can tell when their parents are acting out of the desire to please church members rather than love towards their own children.

It is vital that a child be able to separate their identity as a son or daughter of Jesus, saved by grace through faith, from their identity as a child growing up in the throes of full-time ministry. How can this happen?

One of the things Susan and I have attempted to do, albeit very imperfectly, is to not connect our children's discipleship and spiritual growth to any sort of expectation that we would have of them as a P. K. In fact, we avoid that term in our home like an infectious disease — we are firm believers that terminology shapes our theology. When we attach labels to our children, it unhelpfully shapes the way we parent them.

Our focus in spiritual conversations with our children needs to be about their own hearts and walks with Christ.

While we certainly discuss issues of the church and pray over those ways the ministry is impacting our kids, this is not done with a speech attached to it about the fact that, "You are a pastor's kid wherever you go, and you need to act like it." Our kids intuitively know the unique claims that ministry makes upon them. We do not have to unnecessarily draw their attention and connect their psyches to it.

Here's a question for consideration: Do your children see their identities as being children of God who also happen to have a family in full-time ministry? OR, do they see their primary identities as pastor's kids who must be well-behaved Christians for the sake of dad's job?

Part of having a gospel-based identity is that our children know that we, and most importantly Jesus, love them no matter what daddy's job happens to be. If a child knows that every confession of sin or imperfection revealed is going to be addressed within the context of dad's calling, then we shouldn't be surprised when a culture of shame, secrecy, and fear is bred within a child's heart.

The reason parents and children alike can be honest with themselves, with one another, and with their church family about who they are and what they struggle with is because of the glorious grace of the gospel.

Thus, the gospel must be the primary grounding for kids being raised in the ministry.

PRINCIPLES

PARENTAL BUILDING BLOCKS

When my parents were thinking about building their dream house on a mountain in north Georgia, the process was years in the making. First, they had to pick out a gorgeous piece of hilltop acreage on the side of the mountain. Then, they hired an architect to design the home, thinking about how the layout and space would accommodate future generations of grandchildren. Next came the contractor's work, who spent over a year hauling material up the mountain and then assembling it into something that magically became a beautiful mountain home. Finally, the time came for my parents to move 30 years of stuff out of the old home and into the new.

Now, it would have been utter folly if the first thing mom and dad did in the building process was to take all of their worldly possessions up to the vacant lot and then start finding a place to put them! However, this is precisely what many parents (yes, ministry parents) attempt to do with their kids spiritually: They drag a hodgepodge of spiritual resources and approaches into their parenting plot of land without first putting in the foundational footings and framework.

As we saw in the previous section, the foundation of all parenting must be the gospel. However, before we outfit our "parental home" with various techniques and practices, we need a vision for what this home will look like. With the finished product in view, we can begin to sketch out the principles that will frame this understanding.

Imagine designing your own home. If you're like me, your mind immediately gravitates toward the more exciting and fanciful elements of interior design, but if the house isn't sufficiently framed, wired, and plumbed, you'll never get to experience the beauty of the design as it's properly intended. The same holds true for the family. The gospel is the foundation, but we must pay careful attention to the biblical-theological frame on which to attach our various parenting practices.

There are several no brainer building blocks that surely must comprise the foundation of our children's spiritual lives, including the Bible, the gospel, and of course Jesus himself. However, there are four building blocks and principles that we think are particularly important for those who parent kids in the pastorate.

God-Owned

I had a beater car in college that I treated like, well, a beater. Not only was it old, but it was also free, given to me by my parents because they were probably tired of paying the repair bills. The car took on a certain odor after thousands of miles of road trips, and I think I might have washed it once in three years. I didn't have much incentive to do anything different with the car, not at least until I met Susan. I hadn't paid for the car, so I didn't have much ownership.

How different it was, though, when a few years later I had to borrow my parent's car, a sweet little SUV they bought new, right off the dealer's lot. My mom treated that vehicle like it was her third child — babying, cleaning, and pampering it at every turn. I knew that if I didn't bring it back to her in the exact same condition in which I borrowed it, our relationship as I knew it might be over! The reality of ownership had everything to do with the different ways I treated each car.

The Apostle Paul knew all too well how important this issue of ownership was. The church in Corinth was divided like two college football fan bases on rivalry weekend. It seems that each faction in the church had thrown their support behind their favorite leader: "Paul belongs to *us*!", "Peter is *ours*!", and, "*My* pastor is Apollos!" were the rallying cries of this divided church.

Paul's response to this idea of misunderstood ownership is simple and straight to the point: For we are God's fellow workers. You are God's field, God's building (1 Corinthians 3:9). In other words, the church is God's, the people are God's, and the leaders are God's — everything and everyone belongs to him.

There's a pillar of parenting that is bound up in this truth: Our children really don't belong to us, do they? They are a precious gift from God that he has entrusted to us for a brief time:

> Behold, children are a heritage from the LORD, the fruit
> of the womb a reward. (Psalm 127:3)

We care for, teach, shepherd, and steward "our" little ones — knowing that they are "from the Lord" and that he will one day reclaim them as his own. Ownership confusion, however, is a path to the dark side, particularly for children growing up in ministry.

As we mentioned in the previous chapter, parents can get so locked into creating the model pastor's kid that the child feels used, manipulated, and controlled. Parents forget that their child is a unique image-bearer who holds infinite value to God beyond their earthly function as the offspring of a pastor. In short, they forget that their child belongs to God — not to them.

There is, on the flip side, an equally insidious error when it comes to ownership that also adversely impacts ministry children. This happens when pastors forget that "their" churches are really God's churches. To put it another way, their ministries have become their mistresses.[1]

I recall reading many years ago in Christianity Today the sad story of the unraveling of a well-known pastor's marriage. In this article, his divorcing wife said something striking that speaks to this idea of ownership: "[He], in effect, abandoned our marriage. He chose his priorities, and I have not been one of them."[2]

---

[1] This phrase was first introduced to me in a talk given by Paul Tripp, a fellow pastor and author, at the Sojourn Network Lead Pastors and Wives' Retreat - May, 2018.

[2] Gayle White, Christianity Today, April 29, 1996, https://www.christianitytoday.com/ct/1996/april29/6t5051.html.

While this is only one side of the story, it seems that this pastor had so closely tethered himself to "his" church that he had lost sight of his most fundamental priority — his marriage. What's interesting about this story is that next to his wife, the one person who saw this issue most clearly was his son. Imploring his father to resign his pastorate in order to prioritize his marriage, the son walked away from his dad's church in protest.

Paul Tripp has astutely noted that the self-professed tension that pastors feel between their home lives and church lives is one that is often of their own making. God would never call us, Tripp says, to be faithful in two things that are diametrically opposed to each other — sacrificing one for the other. If we unduly feel this tension, then misplaced ownership may be at the bottom of the resulting carnage.

God has been gracious to gift us with the responsibility of serving two families. Let us remember that both belong to him. Jim Elliot, the famous Christian missionary martyr, once remarked that "wherever you are, be all there." This is good counsel for ministry parents. There are very few things that are truly a pastoral emergency or crisis, regardless of what we may feel. If we are constantly having our family time intruded upon by texts, emails, and social media notifications, then our families will be far less forgiving when real crises arise that require our attention.

Marriage-Prioritized

Coming of age in the 1970s, I've always been a fan of the Brady family — television's iconic sitcom clan. Mike and

Carol, along with the three children that each brought into this new family from previous marriages, comprised a household that had its share of challenges. Sibling rivalries, boyfriend and girlfriend drama, and fights over bedroom space were intertwined with all of the typical complexities that step-parenting brings with it. What was unique about this family, however, was the degree to which Mike and Carol stood united and unified. Try as they might to pit mom and dad against one another, the insoluble bond of the Brady marriage carried the day.

The Brady kids knew they were loved, no doubt — deeply, intimately, and sacrificially. Yet, the security of having the iron-clad bond of Mike and Carol's marriage was like a giant safety net underneath their lives, ready to catch anyone who happened to tumble off of life's tightrope. The children always had the security of their parents' marriage to fall back into.

What was being lived out in that fictional context was in fact a biblical truth: the marital relationship is the most important one in the home. Genesis 2 casts a vision for what God calls the one-flesh relationship: the leaving, cleaving, and prioritizing of marriage. From this marital union flows life, care, work, worship, service, and recreation. The Apostle Paul notes that it is through the husband and wife covenant that the mystery of Christ and the church is lived out and displayed (Ephesians 5).

While this book is not principally about marital health, faithful parenting in a home with two parents can't happen apart from it. After all, any notion that biblically faithful parenting practices can be conceived and applied outside of a healthy relationship between mom and dad is naïve at best and foolish at worst. If the pastor and his wife are parenting their children as a fractured, conflicted, or distant team, there is no organizing and stabilizing center to the home.

Last year, Susan and I got away for a 10-day trip to celebrate our 25th anniversary and 50th birthdays (yes, it was a big year!). As part of this excursion, we participated in a week-long marriage retreat with 10 other pastors and wives. On the first day of camp, we were tasked with having to navigate a high ropes course together as a couple, along with several other (equally terrifying) unity building experiences.

One of our favorite parts of these exercises was the post-activity couple's discussions that took place: Where did we succeed? Where did we struggle? What could we have done differently? It's amazing how many of these discussions brought both our marital and parenting patterns into focus. We never knew that

> **The unity we experienced as a couple empowered us towards unity and togetherness in our parenting.**

cooperation on a 30–feet high rope swing eerily mirrored the way we navigate the complexities of the Chick-Fil-A drive through with our children!

What's the point? We would never have been enlightened to certain patterns in our parenting if we were not able to prioritize our marriage. By pulling away to focus on our oneness, we had a renewed vision and spiritual energy to re-engage our children upon returning home. The unity we experienced as a couple empowered us towards unity and togetherness in our parenting.

Prioritizing your marriage in the midst of ministry goes way beyond date nights and weekends away, of course — although we hope that you are doing those! It's more about having a mutual mindset, a oneness that sets the trajectory for the rest of the family. One of the greatest blessings that we can give our children is security — knowing that even when everything else may be falling apart, mom and dad's relationship is the one constancy in the home.

Here are some daily rhythms that we have found helpful in making sure our marriage does not slide down the list of priorities:

Get Up Early

When we got away for the pastors/wives retreat last summer, one of the blessings was being able to hear the stories and testimonies from other couples. One couple in particular talked about their daily rhythm of getting up at 5:30 AM together to talk, connect, plan, and pray. This was the one time of the day that they could be reasonably assured that they would have a chunk of time just to focus on each other.

While we can't say it's always 5:30 AM or even every day for that matter, we have certainly been blessed as we have begun to imperfectly implement this rhythm. One of the biggest transitions we have had to make as our children have become functioning semi-adults in the house is that we no longer have evening time to connect once the kids go to bed. In fact, we are now the first ones in bed, it seems! Knowing that we have this extended morning time to use as our base of operations has been a lifesaver.

Perfect the Art of Walking

When Susan and I got our Fitbit's a few years ago, we never knew that the primary benefit would be relational! In our desperate attempt to rack up steps by cruising around our neighborhood or the nearby golf course, we found ourselves having all sorts of opportunities to connect and talk together.

Depending upon your living situation and neighborhood, this might be more or less feasible for you. However, we now look forward to a late afternoon or early evening jaunt around the block that allows us to decompress and process the day. Sometimes our kids will go with us as well, allowing family conversations that are more difficult to have at home with all of its distractions.

Go to Sleep at the Same Time

I am a night owl. Susan, on the other hand, makes the roosters look like a late-rising bunch! In combination, those things often resulted in us going to bed at different times early in our marriage. Prior to kids, this wasn't such a big deal because there were countless other opportunities to connect, hang out, and go on dates. When kids arrived, though, this pattern was not only unsustainable, it was also unhealthy.

A couple's sexual relationship is not the only thing in view here, although it's not less than that! The important thing is that since we usually go to bed at roughly the same time, our daily rhythms are more likely to flow together. We are in sync. And, it's much easier to get up at the same time for our morning connection points.

Church-Grounded

Let's be honest: it might seem silly to talk about the importance of the church to the child of a pastor. Isn't that like saying air is important to our breathing? After all, a pastor's kids are *always* around the church. I know ours have been.

Back when Susan was serving part-time as the children's director at our church, there was hardly a family moment where we were *not* at the church. Candy confiscated from the secretary's office; goldfish pilfered from the classrooms; and the occasional Saturday afternoon college football game might be displayed on the sanctuary big screen. The church building was our home away from home.

This is not necessarily what we have in mind, though, when we talk about being "church-grounded." Geo-spatial realities are not the ones we primarily have in view. Hanging around the church all-day may mean that your family is "church-centered," but that does not necessarily mean that it is "church-grounded." There's a big difference between the two.

The Apostle Paul cues us in on this distinction:

I hope to come to you soon, but I am writing these things to you so that, if I delay, you may know how one ought to behave in the household of God, which is the church of the living God, a pillar and buttress of the truth. (1 Timothy 3:15–16)

The church is primarily a family consisting of relationships. The church building is one of the places where the church family gathers to make those relationships happen.

Do your children primarily think about church in terms of its relationships or more in terms of the place that dad works? The former is being "church-grounded"; the latter is more "church-centered."

There are two things in particular that Paul says about the church in these verses which are highly relevant when it comes to raising children who will want to pursue a life-long relationship with Jesus Christ — particularly children whose father happens to be a pastor at the church.

First, Paul says that the church is "a pillar and buttress of the truth." A buttress is something that supports or holds up whatever it is that is resting on it. On one hand, we know that our ultimate authority — God's Word — governs and upholds everything, including the church. However, Paul tells us that this is a reciprocal relationship, as the church actually helps to hold up the Bible by prioritizing it, proclaiming it, and saturating every area of church life in it.

This means that God has designed the church to help hold up the spiritual lives of all Christians. When the church becomes peripheral to a Christian's spiritual life, that means that person is deprived of the blessing of having God's Word preached, taught, lived out, and modeled to them within a diverse, multi-gifted community of people.

Statistics show that the local church has grown increasingly peripheral in the lives of Christians in the United States. As people of mobility and affluence, the pull on our time, energy, and priorities is enormous. While Christians may think that providing their kids an ever-expanding array of travel sports, recreational, and cultural experiences is enriching them, it is oftentimes doing the very opposite by failing to bless and ground them spiritually.

Now, to all of these things, I am sure that every pastor reading this would give a hearty, "Amen!" And, I'm sure you have preached much the same thing to your own children or are planning to. Yet, these truths don't always seem to stick, especially for children growing up in full-time ministry. Sadly, many of these kids will go on to say that the church was more likely to "hold them back" versus "hold them up."

This is why we need to pay particular attention to a second thing Paul says about the church, that it is an *oikos* — literally, "the family of God." One thing I like to remind parents is that the institution of the nuclear family is temporary to this life. Just as there will be no marriage in heaven, neither will there be such a thing as the biological family in eternal glory. Why? Simply put, *we won't need it.*

This is because one of God's chief purposes for the nuclear family in this life is to connect us to and to prepare us for our eternal family — the church. We have a new, eternal family in heaven comprised of God's people, with God as our Father. In fact, we can go as far as to say that *the church is God's forever family.*[3]

We wouldn't dare think about taking our kids out of school for 50% of their school days. That would be an educational and vocational disaster in the making. Why would we think, then, that it would be anything less than a spiritual

---

[3] This quote comes from a talk at our church given by Katie Hughes, the wife of one of our pastors.

disaster to not prioritize something that God says is to be central to the Christian life? If we are not propelling our children towards a lifelong relationship with their forever family, the church, we are leaving them spiritually vulnerable.

What is vitally important for pastors and their wives is to help their children see the church as something much more than an institution, or place of dad's employment, or a purveyor of services and ministries that they must take part in. Rather, the church is its people, and its people are their family. And, ours.

One thing Susan and I have attempted to do is to focus our family conversations less on the politics and organization of the church and more on the people and families of the church. Speaking of the church in the third person (i.e., the church is doing this, the church failed to do that, etc.) is a "no-fly zone" in our house. Community groups, elders, staff, and counseling meetings are not inanimate entities that are all intruding upon and making demands on our home and time. Rather, we try to represent these various groups and ministries as real people who are a part of a community of believers doing life together. We are also eager to talk about how the people of the church give and serve in order for us to have a spiritual family and vocation.

At the same time, however, we do not pretend that families don't have problems, including our own church family. Our experience is that as children grow older, they become intuitively aware of various issues floating around the home and church. To live in denial of those is not healthy. Just because it would be unwise to tell our children everything does not mean that we shouldn't tell them anything. When we do so, let the conversations be honest but discerning.

So, what are we trying to say under this point? Simply this: there is an unhealthy way for the church to be prominent in your children's lives. And, there is a healthy way for the church to be central. Focusing on the spiritual family and relationships versus focusing on the institution will encourage our kids to think about the church rightly.

Family-Focused

It was in the '70s that James Dobson launched his ministry, Focus on the Family. For good reasons, Dobson felt that the nuclear family was under increasing attack from secularism, feminism, materialism, and humanism. The launch of his ministry was a clarion call to Christian families everywhere to re-claim God's authority over their homes and to walk faithfully in His ways, no longer taking a passive posture towards culture.

Today, there is a much different dynamic surrounding the Christian family. It's not that families are neglected; it's that they have assumed center stage. Family vacations, family sports travel, family outings, family activities, and family recreation all conspire to create a sort of idol out of the family unit. It's telling on any given Sunday that the average pastor can look out over his congregation and assume that only about half the people who

It's not that families are neglected; it's that they have assumed center stage.

belong to the church are actually in attendance. Focus on the family, indeed!

We mean something entirely different, though, when we talk about being "family-focused." To use a turn of phrase I once heard from my friend Dave Harvey, what we need to be doing is learning how to "focus our families." Often the twenty-first century-Christian family can function like a lagoon, where every stream, rivet, and brook are flowing in, but no life-giving resources and energy are flowing out. The family becomes a self-contained, independent, autonomous, insular unit that is focused primarily upon its own needs.

Christian history is replete with examples of men who neglected their marriages or families in order to leverage their lives for kingdom purposes. A. W. Tozer's wife, after he died, sadly remarked that "My husband was so close to God, a man of such deep prayer, always on his knees, that he could not communicate with me or our family. No one knew what a lonely life I had, especially after the kids left home." This is an error that many contemporary pastors have vowed not to repeat in their own lives — and for that we are thankful.

However, an equal but opposite error can occur. Instead of sacrificing our families on the altar of ministry success, we now resolve to protect them at all costs. We send them on extended vacations or to go see family without us; we ask them to not attend certain events or meetings; or we live in a neighborhood as far as possible from the church. None of these things will endear your family to the family of God. Indeed, they may very well short-circuit the work of grace God wants to do in and through your family.

We think a healthier paradigm is to prayerfully consider how God would have you "focus your family" for mission. Here are two ways:

Hospitality

One of the things Susan and I have endeavored to do over this previous season is to have a standing night every month or two where we are opening our homes and serving dinner to people who are new to our church. While our children are used to having friends in and out of our home (and us in theirs!), this monthly dinner is distinctive in several ways.

First, this is not our usual lineup of friends and acquaintances, or even our community group members. These are newcomers — fresh faces who our family is meeting for the first time. This communicates to our children that our home is an open place where guests are welcome. Not only that, they come to see that the purpose of our home is not merely to meet the needs of our own family but just as importantly to serve others.

Second, our kids get to meet a plethora of new folks, many of whom are very different from us and who would not naturally be our friends due to age, demographics, or background. They see that the church is indeed a family comprised of diverse people, some of whom have almost nothing in common apart from their fellowship in Jesus Christ.

And, third, our kids are involved in the work and service of getting the home (and their bathroom!) ready to receive these new folks. This helps to position our kids as those who see that God has blessed them and given them certain resources in order for them to serve others. While these monthly dinners can be a veritable beehive of activity for the day or two prior, it is a focused effort that is being done in service to others. The family is on mission.

Service

Another thing that we have done, to some limited success, is to focus our family on an area of service outside of the home. Because we are striving to "do good to everyone, particularly those who are in the household of faith" (Galatians 6:10), we start by picking an area of ministry to the church family.

Our family (Susan and the kids) has developed a bit of a rhythm during certain seasons by serving during one service, and then attending worship the second. This service can take the form of helping in the nursery, teaching a Sunday School class, or leading a youth small group. By doing this, our children are able to see that in healthy families there is reciprocity: a mutual giving and receiving. Our church family, which has been so good to us, is in turn the recipient of our best service and gifts. This also allows our children to see the church as less of an institution, like a school, and more of a family that thrives off of interdependence with one another.

Service can also take place outside of the church family, in service to our neighbors, communities, and cities. Not long ago, Susan organized a group of girls and moms in the church to prepare and serve a meal at the local Ronald McDonald House. Being able to connect our children with a ministry that serves families who have a loved one in the hospital has been an excellent way to demonstrate that the church exists for the good of the community. No longer is the church inward, focusing upon its own needs, but instead is a group of people on mission.

Conclusion

As we have laid out some of the theological principles and foundation pieces for this "parenting in the ministry house" that we are trying to build, it's time to think about what this structure is actually going to look like. What sort of parenting priorities and practices are we going to need to commit ourselves to? It's to this that we now turn.

PROCESS

THREE PRIORITIES OF PARENTING

It's not enough that we merely hear God's instructions to us about our parenting. We need to put his truths into faithful and fruitful practice as well. James, who shoots pretty straight, calls us to "be doers of the word, and not hearers only, deceiving yourselves" (James 1:22). I'm not sure parents were his first target, but we certainly find ourselves in the line of fire on this one!

As we have laid out the philosophy and principles that stand behind what it means to be a faithful parent, in this section we want to leave you with three (that's right, only three!) parenting priorities to purse as doers, not merely hearers, of the Word. Two of these three practices are found in Mark 4; Jude 23 identifies the third. Here are both passages taken together:

> And he [Jesus] said, "The kingdom of God is as if a man should scatter seed on the ground. He sleeps and rises night and day, and the seed sprouts and grows; he knows not how." (Mark 4:26–27)

And have mercy on those who doubt; save others by
snatching them out of the fire; to others show mercy
with fear, hating even the garment stained by the flesh.
(Jude 22–23)

Parents, your child's heart is the field upon which you
want to see the kingdom of God take root. This means that
God will call you to be a Sower, a Snatcher, and a Sleeper in
your children's lives.

The Sowing Parent

Now, Jesus does not leave us clueless about the meaning of
this farming illustration in Mark 4. He reveals the identities of
the farming metaphors in other
verses: the seed is the Word of God
(4:14); the soil is a person's heart
(4:15); and the crop is God's
kingdom (4:26, 28): the rule and
reign of God extended into a
person's heart and life. Applied
specifically to parenting, then, who is the sower? Why, you of
course — the parent!

> **Your child's heart is the field upon which you want to see the kingdom of God take root.**

Parents are often unnerved in thinking about themselves
as the principal sowers of God's Word in their child's life.
Oftentimes, a common refrain from parents is that "I don't
feel equipped; I'm not prepared; I have no seminary training;
I hardly know the Word myself."

Now, these aren't typically the first responses of biblically
trained pastors. After all, we are the Bible experts. We have

tons of experience explaining and teaching the Bible to a variety of audiences — in different languages even! However, we can have our own set of insecurities:

"I can instruct adults, but can I teach kids?"
"How do I impart complex truths to simple people?"
"How deep is too deep?"
"What can my kids handle, or not?"

Now, we will have more to say about this in a moment, but notice something first: there is almost nothing said about the sower. There is no mention of special qualifications. No mention of education, pro or con — no experience is necessary! And, there's no such thing as being over-qualified.

John MacArthur makes this point when he reminds us:

. . . there are no adjectives to describe the sower. . . the sower is anybody who throws seed . . . anybody. There are no [special] qualifications for the sower. The sower is simply somebody who throws seed. . . . It really doesn't matter whether you have a beat-up, tattered burlap seed bag or a designer seed bag.[1]

As fellow parents just like you, we find MacArthur's insights incredibly encouraging. Sometimes, we can become overwhelmed with the many parental hats we are forced to wear: chief administrators; master organizers; event planners; guidance counselors; and child development experts. It's

---

[1] John MacArthur, "The Theology of Sleep," Together for the Gospel 2010, https://t4g.org/media/2010/06/the-theology-of-sleep-mark-4-session-v-2/.

exhausting! Yet, our primary job as parents is to be a doer of the Word by faithfully scattering the seed around the soil of our children's lives and hearts.

This seed, quite simply, is the Word of God. It's the glorious message that God is big, holy, and awesome; that we are loved, but desperate, and sinful; that Jesus is Lord, Savior, and Messiah; and that we are saved by turning to Christ in faith and repentance. Rinse and repeat. Where possible, every day.

Remember, parents: the question is not whether you are a sower. We are all sowers.

Confession: I am a college football fanatic. This passion was instilled early and often in me growing up and provided countless, relationally rich times with my father. Saturdays were punctuated with games at both the beginning and end of the day. . . and for all of the hours in between! Obviously, this was a habit I brought into my adult life as a father, even though I didn't know that I had.

The realization of how powerful sowing can be hit me in a powerful way one day. Susan and I were having a discussion with one of our children about their homework load and household chores that had to be completed over the weekend. This particular child insisted that Sunday afternoon was the only window of time they had to complete these necessities. Incredulous, I asked this child what in the world they were going to be doing all day Saturday. Just as incredulously, they looked back at me like I was crazy, and remarked, "Saturday is for football, dad!"

Again, the issue is not *whether* we are sowing into the lives of our children. Sowers will sow. The issue is *what* we are sowing into the lives of our children. As parents, we are always sowing or planting *something* into our children's lives.

In light of that reality, here are two helpful ways to think about your sowing — proscriptive and prescriptive sowing. While proscriptive sowing are those times that are intentionally created by you as part of a rhythm or discipline, prescriptive sowing happens in response to the needs and circumstances of the moment.

Proscriptive Sowing

Proscriptive sowing could involve: reading a bible story before bed; sharing a devotional at the dinner table (remember, dinner holds a captive audience!); talking about their Sunday school lesson; and praying together before school. Here are three specific suggestions to help you in this area:

1) Use a Book or Devotional Resource

Whether you are having an evening time of family worship or bible discussion during dinner, it is super helpful to have some kind of devotional resource to work from (see Appendix 2). It might be tempting to believe that because you are a pastor, you don't need anything like this. After all, you're talented, knowledgeable, and experienced enough just to "wing it" through that day's lesson.

Wrong.

Or, at least it has been for me. I find that my mind does not transition so easily from sermon prep at the office to family bible reading that night. For some reason, our kids are not as enraptured by the apologetic arguments for including

John 21 as part of John's original gospel as I am! Having a book written specifically for children or students by those more gifted than me in this area has been a lifesaver.

Preaching through a book of the Bible on Sunday mornings makes the sermonic rhythm so much more straightforward, doesn't it? After all, you know ahead of time what you are going to be preaching on that week. The same holds true for family devotions when you are using a resource. It can be challenging enough to pull everyone together for spiritual time as a family without also having to hold your finger in the air to determine the spiritual temperature and message of the day.

2) Bring Them with You

Another proscriptive way to sow God's Word into the lives our children is to include them in a class or study that you are teaching or participating in. It's okay if they don't understand everything that is being taught. Instead of having your child get discouraged or bored, promise them some post-study FroYo or Chick-Fil-A where you can hang out and talk about the study. If you start this early with your kids, it will be much more natural for them to hang with you as they get older. Even when it doesn't appear that our kids are getting anything out of a teaching, they are in fact absorbing it somewhere deep within the recesses of their brains, to be accessed at an opportune time.

I found this to be true for myself. Instead of going to Sunday School class in middle school, I would often attend "big church" with my parents at 1st Presbyterian Chattanooga. Every worship service followed the exact same liturgy. In fact, our pastor, Ben Haden, often said that Presbyterians better do it right the first time because they were going to be doing it the same way for the next 100 years!

Anyway, part of our liturgy at 1ˢᵗ Pres was saying the Apostle's Creed and praying the Lord's Prayer every week for two decades. While no one ever told me that I had to memorize them, memorize them I did — almost by osmosis. The way my mind can still recall and recall these wonderful truths is a testament to something that we often underestimate as parents: the power of bringing them with us.

3) Don't Sideline Your Spouse

One of the grave mistakes I have made (more times than I care to admit) is when I have unintentionally sidelined Susan in the sowing process. Although this has never been a conscious decision, it happens when I begin to have an inflated and distorted view of my leadership in the home: "It's my job to teach the Bible; it's everyone else's job to listen."

Not only is this pride, but it seriously underestimates how much better our devotional times are as a family when my wife participates and helps lead! (Who would have thought that her hanging around the kids all day while I'm at work would make her more sensitive and skilled at communicating with them?)

According to Titus 2, part of my leadership in the home is recognizing Susan's natural calling to pour herself into our children, and for me to actively encourage her in that direction:

Older women likewise are to be reverent in behavior,
not slanderers or slaves to much wine. They are to teach
what is good, and so train the young women to love
their husbands and children. . . (Titus 2:3–4)

Pastors, consult, pray with, receive counsel, and
encourage your wives — and ask them to participate *with* you.
Your sowing will be exponentially better for it.

Prescriptive Sowing

The second kind of sowing that we want to highlight is
that of **prescriptively** planting seeds in the lives of our
children. Deuteronomy 6 describes what this looked like in
the ancient world:

And these words that I command you today shall be on
your heart. You shall teach them diligently to your
children, and shall talk of them when you sit in your
house, and when you walk by the way, and when you lie
down, and when you rise. You shall bind them as a sign
on your hand, and they shall be as frontlets between
your eyes. You shall write them on the doorposts of
your house and on your gates. (Deuteronomy 6:6–9)

Basically, God is telling the Israelites to take whatever
opportunity that presents itself to teach and instruct their
children about the Lord. Whether it be walking, talking,
eating, recreating, or going to bed, God wanted His people to
use their imaginations and ingenuity to see the spiritual in
every situation.

For us, this might mean helping our children to see the roots of a conflict over Legos. It could involve asking questions to encourage your stressed out, homework-saddled student to explore what's going on in their hearts — and what God's Word says about it. And, certainly, it will necessitate taking one of those serendipitous moments on the way to Disney World to contrast the values of God with the values of that raunchy billboard.

We have a favorite reality show that we like to watch as a family. While typically age-appropriate, there have been occasions where an anti-biblical lifestyle, behavioral choice, or value system has been celebrated on screen. Thanks to the joys of DVR, though, we have been able to hit pause and talk about what is happening: "What worldview is being represented? What does the Bible say about this issue? What does the scene we are watching say about God? You? The world?" This has provoked many an entertaining and informative discussion.

There are obviously dozens of situations that present themselves like this on a weekly basis. Everything from a (perceived) injustice incurred at school, to a snub from a friend, or to a provocation from a sibling. All are prescriptive opportunities to respond to an emerging spiritual issue in the hearts of our kids.

The Snatching Parent

When our oldest child, Grace, was about three years old, we were on the Gulf coast having a grand time with extended family. This was such a grand time that one day we momentarily took our eyes off of Grace, who was happily splashing around in the shallow end of the pool. What transpired next seemed to happen in a millisecond. . .

Grace had wandered off into deeper water, and Susan and I both looked up to find her struggling to keep her head above the surface. In the blink of an eye, we were both in the water and at her side. You've never seen two people move faster. I picked Grace up and carried her to safety, as we all cried together in relief.

The point of the story? We didn't wait. We did not scratch our heads and ask if this was a good time for some prescriptive parenting. There was no contemplation about instructing Grace in the finer points of obedience. We didn't let her head go under and her lungs fill with water in order to teach a lesson. We literally snatched her from the jaws of death.

In the passage from Jude we quoted above, the word "snatch" literally means to "seize, pluck, pull, or take by force." In his short little letter, Jude is calling the family of God to arms, so to speak. False teachers have crept into the church under the guise of helping and serving the church. However, like the Trojan Horse left behind by the Greeks, these false teachers are intent on elevating themselves at the expense of others. If left unattended, people's spiritual lives are vulnerable. Jude's command: "save others by snatching them out of the fire."

"Snatching" needs to be a primary commitment of every household. There are times as a parent where we need to directly intervene in order to save our child. There is a God-ordained role for parents that requires them to directly and to immediately remove the threat that has moved against their child. In short, we must be committed to snatching.

One of our children used to require one of those toddler harnesses and leash for us to successfully navigate the rigors of Magic Kingdom. This was completely necessary to ensure that they did not meet their untimely demise by falling off of the Monorail! As parents, physical safety seems to be an instinct that is second nature. We will do anything to protect our children. However, what parents aren't as always in-tune to are the spiritual threats, the kind of threats that move a parent from laissez-faire-ness to spiritual urgency.

Here are two such areas that we believe require particular vigilance and which we are consistently engaged with:

Friends

We want our kids to have friends. We encourage them to be a part of Christian community. We make opportunities for them to have friends over. Our kids do sleepovers and all the rest. So, let's make this clear: we are Pro-Friend! However, we strive to be proactive when it comes to friends by trying to spend just as much time talking with our children about their friends as they do in hanging out with them.

These kinds of conversations tend to be more involved than simply saying, "Hang out with good people; don't hang out with bad people." Parents need to be curious when it comes to the people their kids want to be with. This means asking good questions and asking lots of questions: "What do you like about that person? What concerns you? What sort of things do you talk about when you are together? How did you meet? Who are their parents, and what are they like? And why do you want to hang out with them?"

It is this last question that can be particularly pertinent. Sometimes, a child will gravitate to someone because of some enticement. Other times, your child may have a sincere desire to serve or help someone. This is why they are reaching out to them. However, you won't know what's driving your child's relationships unless you take lots of time to carefully unpack all of the relational dynamics at play. Asking questions is critical in determining whether "snatching" is the most appropriate course of action.

What does snatching look like?

Sometimes, you will be compelled to create boundaries for your child. This might mean forbidding them to see a certain person. Or, it could involve creating a safe context for your child to be with this person in a group, or at your home. For those parents who have children who are temperamentally inclined to be by themselves and are not actively seeking out friends, you might have to take the opposite approach. For one of our children, we set a goal for the number of times they needed to with a group of Christian friends on a weekly basis!

Cell Phones

Another conversation that we find ourselves consistently having with our children revolves around technology. Susan and I sometimes wonder what our childhoods would have been like if we had grown up with a personal computer in the palm of our hands. Our kids don't have to wonder: they are literally living this reality.

Early in our parenting, we had an approach to cell phones that could be succinctly bound up in one word: no. We had seen the dangers and abuses of cell phones wrongly handled by other kids we knew, and it seemed best to steer clear of them altogether.

There came a time in their early to mid-teens, though, when it became obvious that for our children to fully engage their academic, social, and church worlds, they needed personal access to technology. Research done for school; location-tracking features; emails from church and youth group; and instant parental access were just a few of the reasons we began introducing "dumb phones" and then only later smartphones to our children. Again, the principle we discussed before regarding friends applies here as well: we want to be having just as much conversation with our kids about what they are doing on their phones as they are in spending time on their phones themselves. This requires particular vigilance and proactivity because there will be times where the priority of snatching will come to the forefront.

We are fairly restrictive when it comes to social media, particularly in regard to Snapchat and Instagram. We employ an array of filtering software in the home and on all of our devices that place parameters around websites, apps, time spent online, etc. However, no matter how vigilant and thorough you might be, we all know that all technology limits are made to be circumvented, even unintentionally.

This is why we take the time to not only carefully monitor the filtering software we have installed (Disney Circle is our preferred provider), but we also personally go through our children's phones with them. We have also been able to set up their phones so that we can receive all of their ingoing and outgoing texts. This has been a particularly fruitful practice in terms of keeping tabs of our children's network of friends, as we have been able to more proactively address various situations and interactions that have come to light. There have even been a couple of times where we were able to exercise wisdom our children did not have and help to snatch them from unhealthy situations and interactions.

There are a number of other proscriptive and prescriptive things that we have implemented with our children which are drawn from Andy Crouch's book *The Tech-Wise Family* (Appendix 2). We highly recommend this book as you are thinking about how to engage your child in the arena of technology.

The Sleeping Parent

My grandmother made a banana pudding that was truly the envy of all other pudding-makers of the free world. Family members launched missions to discover the secret recipe before Grandma passed away. One lucky soul even managed to secure the secret formula in writing. Yet, no one was ever able to replicate Grandma's banana pudding bliss. It turns out that there was a whole lot of art sprinkled into the pudding that never surfaced in the written recipe.

It's tempting to think that raising children is a lot like re-creating a banana pudding recipe: just mix in the right amounts and the correct set of ingredients and — Voila! . . . you create great, godly, church-going kids. However, it's dangerous when Christians embrace formulas. Take a pinch of proper Education, add a dash of G-rated movies, sprinkle it with a great diet and it produces the next John Piper. Formulas do not always take into account complexities and context and the fact that children are unique image-bearers who have personalized needs.

In reality, Mark 4 sends us in another direction for thinking about how the spiritual seed takes root in our children's hearts. The formula, Jesus says, is pretty simple: the seed is sown, the seed sleeps until stuff happens, then the seed simply sprouts or grows. We are not really sure how it happens. It just happens.

The word for "sprouts and grows" is the Greek term *automatos*, which means "by itself." Jesus is not talking about understanding the scientific and biological processes that results in the growth of life. It's much simpler and far more profound. He's saying farmers can create the conditions and plant the seed, but they can't make anything happen. They are powerless to make the seed grow — it does so from other sources outside of themselves.

It's not hard to see how this applies to parenting. When it comes to our kids, we don't create the seed or cause it to take root. We can't change our child's heart or make the kingdom of God take root. Only God can do that, which, by the way, is why we do pray, "Lord, let your kingdom come in the life of my child."

So, what does this mean for this third category of parenting priorities? Simply this: We sow hard, we snatch when necessary, and then we get a good night's sleep. In other words, there is a point where every parent simply needs to just trust God and go to bed. Spiritually speaking, parents must learn to sleep and rest, confident that God will animate the seed and make it grow.

One of the primary ways, if not the primary way that parents can undergird their posture of sleeping is through

There is a point where every parent simply needs to just trust God and go to bed.

prayer. Let's be honest: prayer oftentimes seems like it's the most inefficient thing we can do. Particularly for a capitalistic, entrepreneurial sort that we Americans tend to be, prayer can be seen as a nice "add on" to the real task of parenting. This, of course, is a deception.

The Sleeping Parent is the Praying Parent. Nothing communicates more clearly to our souls that we are not in charge than to be in a humble posture of prayer. While we have not been as faithful and consistent in praying for our kids as we would want to be, the most prayerful seasons have been the ones where we have been the most needful.

CONCLUSION

When we first became parents over 20 years ago, Christian literature was rife with resources that purported to help mom and dad parent their children, "God's way." No doubt, some of this material was helpful. Yet, it also put out a grace-less vibe that fueled unhealthy guilt over the fact that we were not doing it the way the experts said to do it.

We hope and pray that this will not be your experience in reading this book. We are neither parenting experts nor holy practitioners. However, we are saved sinners whom God has been pleased to bless with the great privilege of parenting.

Parents, we must all remind ourselves of these truths: Sowing is important, but not decisive. Snatching is critical, but it is never determinative. While we can exert much influence over our kids, we can never seize control of their decisions for or against God. This wonderful news liberates us from worry, manipulation, and the weird ways we can try to manufacture spiritual outcomes in our children's lives.

Sow much, snatch when necessary, sleep continually, and trust the promises of God for your kids.

PRACTICES

APPENDICES

APPENDIX ONE

HOW TO TAKE A FAMILY VACATION

No ministry family can survive long without a clear, well-thought-out rhythm of rest, time off, and vacation. I highly recommend Rusty McKie's book on *Sabbaticals* for a well-grounded theology of rest and renewal.[1]

In terms of intentionally integrating rest and renewal with your children, the age-old family vacation still holds great potential for connection, care, memory making, and family bonding.

One of the things that getting away together as a family has done is that it has enabled our children to establish an identity that is independent of dad's professional vocation. Over time, home life can become too wedded to church life, in a creepy, cultic kind of way. Establishing rhythms where every conversation and outing revolves around church activities is an important part of this re-identification process.

---

[1] Rusty McKie, *Sabbaticals: "How-To" Take a Break from Ministry before Ministry Breaks You* (Louisville, TN: Sojourn Network, 2018).

Here are a few suggestions for how to plan and to take a great family vacation:

- Sit down with your spouse and a calendar and try to forecast the ministry year from start to finish. Make sure to write down all of the known ministry events and happenings and calendar them accordingly.

- Do the same thing with your children's school and extra-curricular schedules, noting particularly those times where you have blocks of time to pull away.

- We would recommend "blocking" at least part of your vacation time in order to have a more extended time away (more than a week). Sometimes, we find it difficult to get into a vacation rhythm until the second or third day, particularly if we are coming off of an intense, busy ministry season. Our brains know that they are on vacation, but it seems it takes our bodies and physiological responses a bit longer to wind down.

- Try your best to get out of town. We have found that the times we have tried to "stay-cation" often do not work well. When we stay at home, the pattern of our daily lives tends to take over, and it can be tempting to connect with our routines, habits, and networks. It also makes it more difficult to bond as a family when friends, neighbors, and church folks are not themselves "stay-cating!"

- Ask around to see if anyone has second homes or vacation rentals that they would allow you to use for cheap. Or, free! Sometimes, different hotel chains will run specials where you can sign up for their credit card and get a certain number of nights free or deeply discounted.

- Establish some family rhythms and activities during your vacation times that you can remember, celebrate, and return to year after year. For more specific ideas, see Appendix 4 on Ebenezering with your kids.

APPENDIX TWO

TECH-WISING YOUR HOME

It's not whether or not you have a "philosophy of technology" in your home — everyone does. The issue is whether you have a wise one that is well-thought-out and reasoned or an implicit one that unknowingly governs technological interactions in your home in an unhealthy way.

The book we have found most helpful in helping us think through our approach to technology in the home is Andy Crouch's *The Tech-wise Family*. While we highly recommend you read this marvelous little book in its entirety, here are Crouch's 10 Tech-Wise Commitments for his own family that we have found enormously helpful:[1]

1. We develop wisdom and courage together as a family.

---

[1] Excerpted from *The Tech-Wise Family* by Andy Crouch. ©2017. Used by permission of Baker Books, a division of Baker Publishing Group. www.bakerpublishinggroup.com.

2. We want to create more than we consume. So we fill the center of our home with things that reward skill and active engagement.

3. We are designed for a rhythm of work and rest. So one hour a day, one day a week, and one week a year, we turn off our devices and worship, feast, play and rest together.

4. We wake up before our devices do, and they "go to bed" before we do.

5. We aim for "no screens before double digits" at school and at home.

6. We use screens for a purpose, and we use them together, rather than using them aimlessly and alone.

7. Car time is conversation time.

8. Spouses have one another's passwords, and parents have total access to children's devices.

9. We learn to sing together, rather than letting recorded and amplified music take over our lives and worship.

10. We show up in person for the big events of life. We learn how to be human by being fully present at our moments of greatest vulnerability. We hope to die in one another's arms.

APPENDIX THREE

10 RESOURCES FOR FAMILY DEVOTIONALS AND TEACHING

1

Family Worship
Donald S. Whitney

2

A Neglected Grace: Family Worship in the Christian Home
Jason Helopoulos

3

Family Worship Bible Guide
Joel R. Beeke

4

Family Worship (Family Guidance)
Joel R. Beeke

5

*Training Hearts, Teaching Minds: Family Devotions
Based on the Shorter Catechism*
Starr Meade

6

Family Shepherds: Calling and Equipping Men to Lead Their Homes
Voddie Baucham Jr.

7

The Ology: Ancient Truths, Ever New
Marty Machowski

8

*The Gospel Story Bible: Discovering Jesus in the Old and
New Testaments*
Marty Machowski

9

Small Talks on Big Questions (vol. 1)
Susan Thompson
Small Talks on Big Questions (vol. 2)
Selah Helms

10

The Child's Story Bible
Catherine F. Vos

APPENDIX FOUR

RELATIONAL RHYTHMS WITH YOUR KIDS

Feasting

Mike Cosper's book, *Recapturing the Wonder* has a really great section on how to pull off a family feast.[1] You might try making a certain kind of food or dish that you only eat on special occasions, like Christmas, Thanksgiving, or birthdays. Rehearse God's goodness and what you are thankful for during these times. Then, whenever your family pulls out that special recipe, there is an edible reminder of the grace of God in years past.

Foodie Outings

Our house is in walking distance of a local FroYo joint, and we have taken full advantage to consume countless cups of

---

[1] Mike Cosper, *Recapturing the Wonder: Transcendent Faith in a Disenchanted World* (Downers Grove, IL: IVP, 2017).

this deliciousness. It's a rhythm that has allowed us to connect as a family. In addition, there are a set of eateries and hotspots that we return to year after year at our usual vacation spots. Culinary connection points are some of the most effective in terms of building life-long bonds.

"Ebenezering"

"Raising an Ebenezer" means making or establishing some sort of marker by which you can remember and celebrate God's goodness. A friend of ours made a bookcase for us in honor of his kids being a part of our youth group. He said that every time we looked at it and thought about all that went into making and staining it, we should think about the way God used us to build into his own kid's lives.

For us, arts, crafts, and various kinds of displays serve as testimonies to God's grace. For example, the church threw us a surprise going-away celebration for our sabbatical about 10 years ago. One of the mementos that we took home that day was a giant banner with a picture of our family on it, with a word of affirmation affixed to it. We hung this in our garage and it still serves as a reminder to the faithfulness of God during that season.

Media

For the Gilberts, particular videos and digital pictures we have made mark special events and seasons. Our kids love to go through these different media types and laugh, celebrate, cry, and rehearse our history together. While we don't want to make our screens the centerpieces of our homes, leveraging media around memories can pull the family together at strategic times.

Parting Thoughts on Relational Rhythms

Parents, we must remember that we cannot NOT establish relational rhythms in our homes with our children. The question is, what will those relational rhythms be? Before you embark on implementing any new practices, it might be helpful to take an inventory of your current rhythms. Getting a clear picture of what you are currently doing might help give you clarity about what you want to do going forward.

ACKNOWLEDGMENTS

This book is the fruit of an intimate, spiritual partnership with the greatest woman I have ever known — Susan Ward Gilbert. Her emotional, physical, mental, and spiritual investment in the hearts and lives of our four children has been nothing short of life-giving. Sweetheart, I thank the Lord for the 27 years of grace that God has poured out on me through our marriage and family. You have truly been salvation for all of us.

I am beyond thankful for the four children that God has blessed us with: Gracie (20); Maggie (19); Jack (16); and Virginia (13). Despite our best efforts to give them a "normal" childhood, I know that having a pastor as a father has thrust them into the public stage in ways that have been hard, difficult, and challenging. To the "Fab Four," I just want to say that I love each of you very much and am eternally thankful to God that you are each walking with Jesus Christ.

These kinds of books don't "just happen" apart from the folks who pour themselves into these projects. My gratefulness and thanks go out to Ronnie Martin and Casey

Smith particularly in serving as the editors, collaborators, and chief encouragers in this work. I also want to thank my good friend, Dave Harvey, who first gave me the opportunity to write about parenting in full-time ministry as part of a small contribution to the Am I Called blogsite. Dave, your input, edits, and suggestions for those initial blog posts served as the framework for this book.

Finally, thanks to each and every pastor and ministry worker in the Sojourn Network for your friendship and faithful partnership in the gospel. May this book, in some small way, serve you as you attend to the most important spiritual relationships in your life: your family.

ABOUT THE AUTHOR

Paul Gilbert is the Lead Pastor of Four Oaks Community Church in Tallahassee, FL, where he has served on the pastoral staff for 23 years. He is a co-author of the book *Letting Go: Rugged Love for Wayward Souls*, and serves as a Strategist in the Sojourn Network. Paul holds a B.A. in Speech Communication (University of Tennessee), an M.Div. and an M.A. in Marriage and Family Therapy from Reformed Theological Seminary, and a Ph.D. from Florida State University in Marriage and Family. Paul and his wife Susan have been married for 27 years and have four children: Gracie (20); Maggie (19); Jack (16); and Virginia (13).

ABOUT SOJOURN NETWORK

Throughout the pages of the New Testament, and especially in the book of Acts, we observe a pattern: men and women, through prayer and dependence of God and empowered by the Spirit, are sent by God (often through suffering) to spread the Word of the Lord. As this great news of new life in Christ spread into the neighboring cities, regions, provinces, and countries, gatherings of new believers formed into local communities called churches. As these gatherings formed by the thousands in the first century, the early church — taking its cue from the scriptures — raised up qualified, called, and competent men to lead and shepherd these new congregations.

Two-thousand years later, God is still multiplying his gospel in and through his church, and the Good Shepherd is still using pastors to lead and shepherd God's people. In Sojourn Network, we desire to play our part in helping these pastors plant, grow, and multiply healthy churches.

We realize that only the Spirit can stir people's hearts and bring them into community with other believers in Jesus. Yet, by offering the pastors in our network a strong vision of planting, growing, and multiplying healthy churches and by providing them with thorough leadership assessment, funding for new churches and staff, coaching, training, renewal, and resources, we can best steward their gifts for the benefit and renewal of their local congregations.

Since 2011, our aim at Sojourn Network has been to provide the care and support necessary for our pastors to lead their churches with strength and joy — and to finish ministry well.

OTHER "HOW-TO" BOOKS

Here are the current books in the "How-To" series. Stay tuned for more.

Healthy Plurality = Durable Church: "How-To" Build and Maintain a Healthy Plurality of Elders by Dave Harvey

Life-Giving-Groups: "How-To" Grow Healthy, Multiplying Community Groups by Jeremy Linneman

Charting the Course: "How-To" Navigate the Legal Side of a Church Plant by Tim Beltz

Redemptive Participation: A "How-To" Guide for Pastors in Culture by Mike Cosper

Filling Blank Spaces: "How-To" Work with Visual Artists in Your Church by Michael Winters

Before the Lord, Before the Church: "How-To" Plan a Child Dedication Service by Jared Kennedy with Megan Kennedy

Sabbaticals: "How-To" Take a Break from Ministry before Ministry Breaks You by Rusty McKie

Leaders through Relationship: "How-To" Develop Leaders in the Local Church by Kevin Galloway

Raising the Dust: "How-To" Equip Deacons to Serve the Church by Gregg Allison & Ryan Welsh

Parenting in the Pastorate: "How-To" Faithfully Raise Kids in Full-Time Ministry by Paul Gilbert

Healthy Plurality = Durable Church: "How-To" Build and Maintain a Healthy Plurality of Elders by Dave Harvey

Have you ever wondered what separates a healthy church from an unhealthy church when they have the same doctrine (and even methods) on paper? The long-term health and durability of a church simply cannot exceed the health of her elders who lead, teach, shepherd, and pray the church forward. Therefore, building and maintaining a healthy plurality of elders is the key to durability. Yet a healthy plurality is a delicate thing working through hardship and the difficulties of relationship while pursuing the noble task of eldership. If you wish to grow deeper in your theology of eldership to lead with a healthy, biblical vision of plurality, then this is your "How-To" guide.

Life-Giving-Groups: "How-To" Grow Healthy, Multiplying Community Groups by Jeremy Linneman

Cultivate life-giving, Christ-centered communities. After many years of leading small groups and coaching hundreds of small group leaders, pastor and writer Jeremy Linneman has come to a bold conviction: Community groups are the best place for us — as relational beings — to become mature followers of Christ. This short book seeks to answer two questions: How can our community groups cultivate mature disciples of Christ? And how can our groups grow and multiply to sustain a healthy church? Whether you are new to community groups or tired from years of challenging ministry, *Life-Giving Groups* is a fresh, practical invitation to life together in Christ.

Charting the Course: "How-To" Navigate the Legal Side of a Church Plant by Tim Beltz

Planting a church? It's time to plot the course toward legal validity. Church planting is overwhelming enough before dealing with the legal and business regulations of founding a church. *Charting the Course* is for anyone, at any experience level to learn how to navigate the legal side of planting a church.

Redemptive Participation: A "How-To" Guide for Pastors in Culture by Mike Cosper

Our culture is confused. And so are we. It's not just you or them. It's all of us. But we can move past confusion and into a place of careful discernment. *Redemptive Participation* brings awareness to the shaping forces in our current culture and how to connect these dynamics with our teaching and practice.

Filling Blank Spaces: "How-To" Work with Visual Artists in Your Church by Michael Winters

In the beginning, the earth was empty. Blank spaces were everywhere. *Filling Blank Spaces* addresses a topic that usually gets blank stares in the church world. But Winters is a seasoned veteran of arts ministry and has developed a premier arts and culture movement in the United States, without elaborate budgets or celebrity cameos. Instead, this guide gives a "How-To" approach to understanding visual art as for and from the local church, steering clear of both low-brow kitsch and obscure couture. If you are ready to start engaging a wider, and often under-reached, swath of your city, while awakening creative force within your local church, then this book is for you.

Before the Lord, Before the Church: "How-To" Plan a Child Dedication Service by Jared Kennedy with Megan Kennedy

Is child dedication just a sentimental moment to celebrate family with "oohs and ahhs" over the babies? Or is it a solemn moment before God and a covenanting one before the local church? Kennedy explains a philosophy of child dedication with poignant "How-To" plan for living out a powerful witness to Christ for one another and before the watching world. Whether you are rescuing various forms of child dedication from sentimentalism or perhaps sacrament, this book will guide you to faithful and fruitful ministry honoring God for the gift of children while blessing your church.

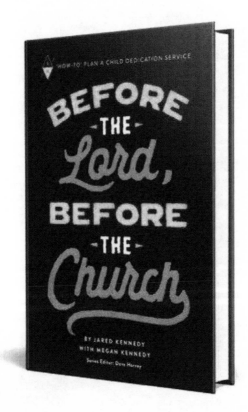

Sabbaticals: "How-To" Take a Break from Ministry before Ministry Breaks You by Rusty McKie

Are you tired and worn out from ministry? Isn't Jesus' burden supposed to be light? In the pressure-producing machine of our chaotic world, Jesus' words of rest don't often touch our lives. As ministry leaders, we know a lot about biblical rest, yet we don't often experience it. The ancient practice of sabbath provides ample wisdom on how to enter into rest in Christ. *Sabbaticals* is a guide showing us how to implement Sabbath principles into a sabbatical as well as into the ebb and flow of our entire lives.

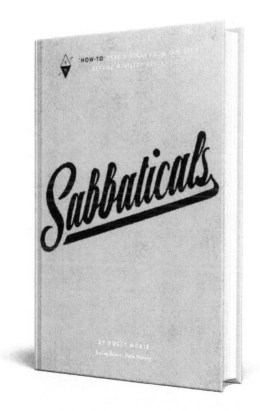

Leaders through Relationship: "How-To" Develop Leaders in the

Local Church by Kevin Galloway

The church needs more godly leaders. But where do they come from?
Some people read leadership books in a season of rest and health. But if
we're honest, most often we read leadership books when we're frazzled,
when we see the problems around us but not the solutions. If you're feeling
the leadership strain in your church, let Kevin Galloway show you a way
forward, the way of Jesus, the way of personally investing in leaders who
then invest in other leaders—because making an intentional plan to
encourage and train leaders, is not a luxury; it's mission critical, for your
health and the health of your church.

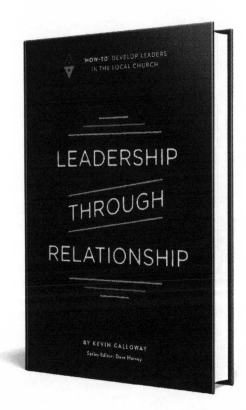

Raising the Dust: "How-To" Equip Deacons to Serve the Church by Gregg Allison & Ryan Welsh

How we organize our churches might seem insignificant, but it's not. In his letter to the church in Rome, the apostle Paul climbs great, theological mountains. But he also explores the valleys where we live our lives. Love one another with affection, he writes. Outdo one another in showing honor, he writes. Contribute to the needs of the saints and show hospitality. This is the calling of all Christians. And God intends that deacons lead the way. How is your church doing? *Raising the Dust* will help you better understand who deacons are, what God expects them to do, and how they bless the body of Christ.

Parenting in the Pastorate: "How-To" Faithfully Raise Kids in Full-Time Ministry by Paul Gilbert

Parenting is hard work, especially when everyone is watching. The Lord requires that those who lead his church also excel at leading their own families. In fact, the ability to manage one's household, Paul writes, is a prerequisite. But how do we love our children well given all the demands pastors face? Have you ever left the office for home with your sermon printed, all your emails answered, your members prayed for, your stack of books read, and your staff encouraged? Probably not. Paul Gilbert has been there. And in *Parenting in the Pastorate*, he shows weary pastor-parents that the same God who gives us churches and children also gives us grace—grace that forgives our failures and empowers our parenting.

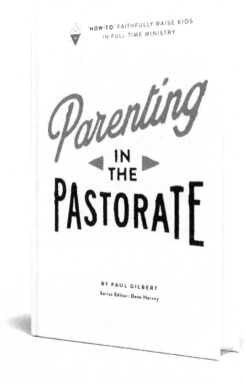

SOJOURN NETWORK "WHITE PAPERS"

Sojourn Network is committed to rigorous, biblical thinking about topics that matter. Our online Sojourn Network store (www.sojournnetwork.com/store) has "white papers" that are free to download.

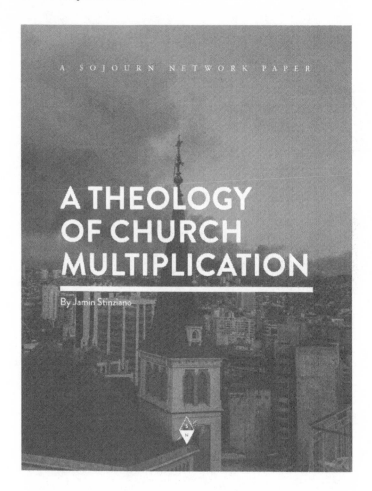

Visit www.sojournnetwork.com/store to download this resource for free.

A SOJOURN NETWORK PAPER

TO REST IS HUMAN:

ESCAPING EXHAUSTION BY TRUSTING, STOPPING, AND ENJOYING

By Daniel Montgomery

Visit www.sojournnetwork.com/store to download this resource for free.

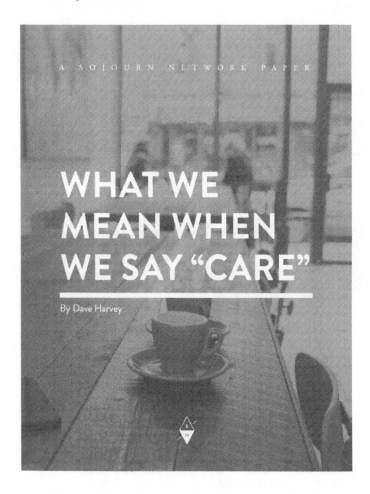

Visit www.sojournnetwork.com/store to download this resource for free.

A SOJOURN NETWORK PAPER

WHAT "NETWORK" MEANS TO US

By Dave Harvey

Visit www.sojournnetwork.com/store to download this resource for free.

Visit www.sojournnetwork.com/store to download this resource for free.

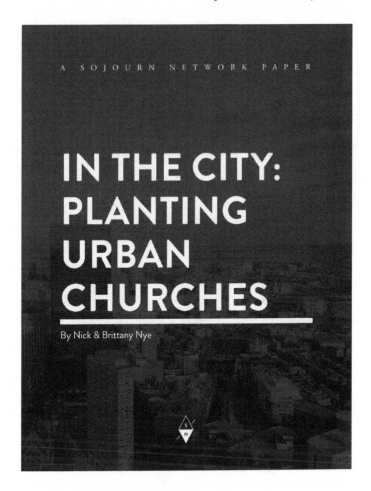

A SOJOURN NETWORK PAPER

IN THE CITY: PLANTING URBAN CHURCHES

By Nick & Brittany Nye

Visit www.sojournnetwork.com/ store to download this resource for free.

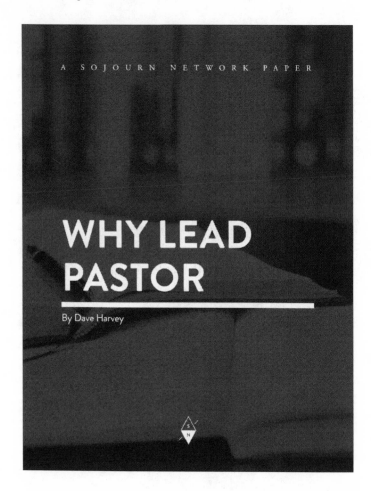

A SOJOURN NETWORK PAPER

WHY LEAD PASTOR

By Dave Harvey

Visit www.sojournnetwork.com/store to download this resource for free.

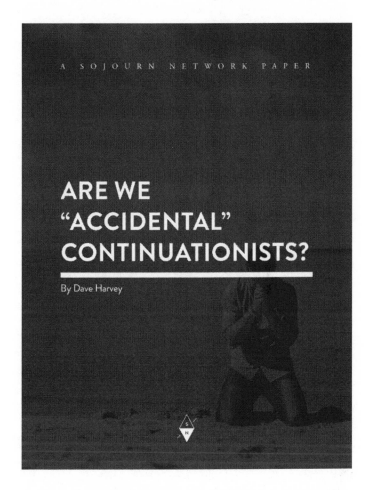

A SOJOURN NETWORK PAPER

ARE WE "ACCIDENTAL" CONTINUATIONISTS?

By Dave Harvey

Visit www.sojournnetwork.com/store to download this resource for free.

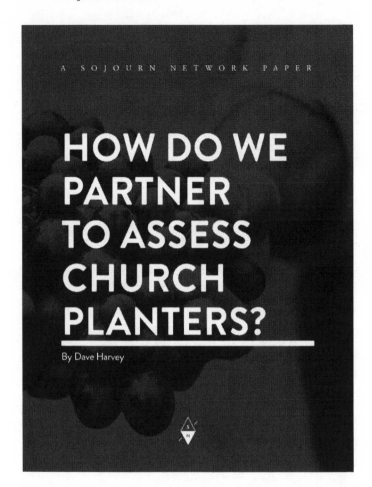

Visit www.sojournnetwork.com/store to download this resource for free.

Visit www.sojournnetwork.com/store to download this resource for free.

Made in the
USA
Lexington, KY